Self Discipline

Guide to develop mental toughness and unseen willpower

Table of Contents

Introduction

Is it really possible to improve my self-discipline? Can I really make a change in my life? These are some of the questions I normally encounter, the answer is yes! But it solely depends on you to do it!

You will experience improvement as soon as you start working on yourself! Your improvement will be in direct proportion to how much time and effort you decide to invest in your transformation. A partial effort will generate a partial result! Take care of your mind and your mind will take care of yourself!

This book contains the quickest and easiest methods for improving self-discipline. In this book you will find methods that will work fast, we will use a direct and powerful approach for improving self-discipline and developing incredible willpower. You will learn more than you anticipate. The systems in this book will give you the techniques, insights, and tips to create or re-create this "skill". Yes! I do consider self-discipline to be a skill. It is developed by hours and hours of practice. No one comes into the world with it. Improving self-discipline, like improving any other skill is a matter of education, practice, and patience.

Most of us learned about self-discipline from friends, from people that we admire, from parents or relatives. Others learned about self-discipline from school, sports, passions, or maybe their own intuition. Unfortunately, there are still a lot of people out there who don't know how to achieve self-discipline and how it really works. By reading this book you will learn how to develop your self-discipline and realize what you need to drop. Soon you will understand many tools and concepts to unravel this mystery. You will be amazed at how quickly and easily this self-discipline system works.

The trademarks that are used are without any consent, and the publication of the trademark is without permission or backing by the trademark owner. All trademarks and brands within this book are for clarifying purposes only and are the owned by the owners themselves, not affiliated with this document.

Chapter 1 - Getting Started With Developing Self-Discipline

"One thing at a time!" Is the best advice that I received from a friend when I was young. It's one of the best concepts I prefer you take into consideration when making a behavior change. Do not skip from one chapter to chapter when studying this book!

I will start by talking about beliefs and how they form our character. I normally hear people make statements like: I will lose my freedom if I start doing X. I will lose my clarity, I will lose my sense of fun, I'll be drowning by problems and responsibilities or I'll put too much pressure on myself. Most of the beliefs that I have highlighted above are false. We all have a crazy side to our personality. That part is trying to resist being organized or any kind of structure. This rebel side of our personality naturally comes from childhood.

REMEMBER THIS!

Part of your mind is not willing to take action, to be organized or to self-discipline.
We are all seeking comfort at some level. This is a condition of being human. Let's call this "dark" side of your personality Lusi. Lusi doesn't want you to gain control over your thoughts, desires, and ambitions. Lusi not only knows all your weaknesses, fears and insecurities but also

know how to use them against you. This dark side of yours, named Lusi, when it enters inside your plans it employs every method of manipulation available to keep you from following the program that you laid out for yourself.

Five bad habits that you need to get rid off

1. Cynicism
2. Negativism
3. Resistance
4. Fear
5. Procrastination

1. Cynicism

A cynical person has the tendency to question everything and even not trust their own instinct. They are inclined to question the goodness and the value of everything. In life, you will often find yourself in a situation that is uncomfortable or just unpleasant. Getting a new job, dealing with heartbreak, loss of dear ones, those are a couple of things that a cynical person will deal with. Cynical people usually see those facts as being bad even though they are just facts. Cynical persons such as pessimistic friends, or negative relatives should be avoided at all costs. Cynicism is very contagious, you won't realize when you are been hooked to this habit or a change of the way of thinking if you don't pay attention to it. The cynic is very smart at pointing out why a plan, choice or idea won't work or even not worth trying out.

REMEMBER THIS!

There is a part of you that will always resist discipline and being organized! Deal with it! Luci is one of the forces that are inside of us and wants all of us to become cynic. "It's too hard for me". "I will try it when I will have more free time." "I'm too tired for doing this today." "Requires too much effort." And the list can be even longer than this.

Solution to cynicism

Belief in yourself! Have the trust that you can make it and you will! I found the confidence to be one of the single "antidotes" that exist to escape cynicism. Have faith in your ability to change yourself and to improve. Nobody is perfect, but first, you have the faith you can change just one small thing. If you concentrate on being perfect you just allow Luci in your mind. However, if you concentrate just on the belief that you want to implement you will get rid of the cynicism in a very short period of time.

Being focused on achieving goals, in the present moment and on concrete self-talk is your first line of defense against Luci. Luci's efforts will fade away if you start implanting those three suggestions right away. You will feel a flow of strength the very first time you challenge yourself and Luci.

2.   Negativism

This is another big problem that people deal with. During your first attempts trying to get your self-discipline, you have to create and maintain a positive attitude. Another tool that Luci has is to spotlight all the negative events in your life. I.e Your car broke down, your girlfriend is leaving you, you parent have health problems and so on. It hurts or maybe you can feel the pain just by reading those words. Deal with it! Deal with everything that appears in your life, prepare your "emotional fitness"! Luci will try to direct your attention toward everything unpleasant about people around you, places and actions taking place in your environment. You will find yourself asking a question like, " Do I take action"?

Well, that is a good question, " Do I take action"? After all, you are tired. You had a long day at the job, your boss yelled at you. Your shoes are too tight and you don't have money to change them. All those reasons listed should represent reasons to take action instead of putting things aside. There are cancer-causing food additives in what you eat. Your friends are going out and have fun, do I take action?

Also, this brings down a couple of things such as, what do you want and maybe more important than the first one why you want it?

Negativism also searches for reasons to support negative attitudes, or better say, Luci, is searching for them. Whatever you tell yourself, either negative or positive your subconscious mind will believe it. Your subconscious mind will take it as it is. It simply believes whatever you tell it. Besides that, your subconscious mind will find reasons to support what you are thinking and also to prove your right even if the belief is wrong and not supporting your goals.

To resume it, *you create attitude and actions by what you imagine.* Imagine reading this book is bullshit or wrong and your mind will find reasons why it is. Interesting, right? Pay attention to your thoughts.

REMEMBER THIS!

You will always have to put your feet down! Without taking action you won't get   control over yourself and your thoughts!

Solution to Negativism

Always bear in mind that your attitude has everything to do with your success. Believe that in every situation you are in, there is a good side and a solution to it.

You have the power to decide on what to focus on. You always have to be positive minded. Create your own attitude and it will reflect your behavior. Another important thing is that your attitude is always in your control! You DECIDE if you want to be happy or sad by the interpretation you give to the events in your life! Be aware of how you view the events in your life. A strong positive attitude is your antidote to Luci's tactic to get your mind!

Luci wants to drift you away from your path. There will be always a lot of options and things to try. Keep your mind only on one thing. Luci will try to remind you of all that's wrong in your life or in the world. On the surface, a negative attitude doesn't seem related to self-discipline, but I can assure you it is.

3. Resistance

Resistance is contributed and created by Cynicism and Negativism. Resistance will appear in your life in different forms. "Maybe this book won't help me get more self-discipline, I should stop reading it". "I'm too old for this kind of things." "I'm not smart enough to understand it and to apply it into my life." Luci is trying to make you consider that the problem is within yourself. You are the problem, you and your conditions. You somehow lack the ability to turn the situation you are in right now, in something better.

Resistance is commonly met. Your intellect will tell you that lots of people have tried this kind of things, but "you are different". "You are not like them".

REMEMBER THIS!

You are in control of your mind and your thoughts!

Solution to Resistance

First, you need to believe in your ability to get knowledge. It's not that hard to acquire new skills and knowledge. Believe in your ideas and that they will work for you. Some of the techniques in this book have been around for centuries. Other techniques are from recently developed psychological approaches to self-management.

Words will help you take action, positive words will sculpt your behavior. When Luci tries to make you resist your ideas and dreams stop for a while and say to yourself: "Nothing is going to pull me away from my path. It's my decision to take action and I'm in control of myself".

4. Fear

Developing self-discipline requires self-knowledge. Self-knowledge requires that you constantly engage in self-examination. Self-examination creates anxiety and anxiety is created by fear. Like a forgotten treasure self-knowledge requires you to dig deep before you can really get to the gold. Fear is another bad habit that will try to get you off track.

Emotional stones in your subconscious mind include many events and situation that you just have left buried. Those stones contain the keys to why certain parts of you refuse to take action and to cooperate in your efforts to improve yourself. This applies to everything in your life. Whether we are talking about dieting, running a business or maintaining a relationship.

Be aware of this emotional stones. It is very important to identify what is hindering you from being the best. Naturally, you will experience discomfort and that will create fear. That feeling of fear is created by Luci.

Luci at the back of your mind will try and feed you with negative thoughts like: "Maybe it's going to hurt if I'll do all those things." "Maybe that person is going to refuse me if I approach him/her." "Maybe it's not a good idea to invest my money in this business." "Maybe lifting weight will make me be too muscular." "Maybe I should not tell that person what I really think." I think you got the point! The list can go even longer than this.

It may not make sense at this point, but hold on. As you subject yourself to self-examination, Luci will try to divert you from your best. This happens especially when you haven't yet developed self-discipline.

REMEMBER THIS!

Fear does not really exist at the present moment! It's as a result of something that happened in the past (like a "failure") or something that might happen in future. In actual sense, fear doesn't exist.

Solution to Fear

Fear will never go away from your life! It will always be there! It's based on the cause and effect principle but with a negative implication that will result into a pain in your life. In life, the actions you take are as a result of cause and effect. The actions that you will take on this journey of self-discovery might get you in uncomfortable situations.

Be willing and ready to experience discomfort in your life. Keeping in mind that discomfort will quickly transform into a wonderful feeling of accomplishment as you enjoy the success that results from your actions. The resulting success will get you away from that feeling of fear.

When you find yourself trying to escape a situation of discomfort in your life, always remember the concept of Luci at the back of your mind who's the main objective is to derail you from accomplishing self-discipline. Ask yourself: "Is this the right thing to do?" or "Is this lack of action caused by fear?"

5. Procrastination

Procrastination is the last bad habit that we are going to talk about. It revolves around postponement of activities, "I will do that later", "there is enough time for that task next week." This is purely another creation of Luci. Procrastination manifests itself also through the notion that: just waiting for the right moment. Luci will try to convince you on that notion for instance in the following way; "I can't be working on that business until I have enough time," "I can't start losing weight until I'm uncomfortable." Sounds familiar? I guess the answer is yes because I have been in that situation myself.

The line "I don't have time to do it right now" is the most used for procrastination. We all have the same number of hours per day.

Depends just on how we decide to use our time. What you ***choose*** to do with your time is the most important thing. Your choices will shape your results.

REMEMBER THIS!

Time is the only asset that you have. Be careful with how you manage your time to get the most out of it!

Solution to Procrastination

First of all, it's important to admit to yourself that you are putting aside important things that you have to do. The idea is to recognize whether that delay is legitimate or it's just another excuse to keep you away from work. Procrastination will keep you away from being and becoming the best version of yourself. Start by setting a definitive goal for yourself! Having a purpose will help you act properly in any moment of the day! That's how you put bricks into building self-discipline.

Chapter 2 – Self Talk Importance

Having an understanding of how Luci operates is very important. Don't see Luci (or bad behaviors) as an enemy. Such thinking will put you into a combative state of mind. Will drag you into an inner conflict with yourself. This will make you fight with yourself.

Acknowledging a bad behavior is the first step that you have to take in order to improve yourself. Acknowledging what you are doing "bad" and is leading you away from your path will make implementing the solution easier. You need to thoroughly familiarize yourself with the power of self-talk.

Probably this is not the first time you are hearing about the importance of self-talk. Although a lot of people know how important the concept of self-talk is, few people actually know how to use it. Self-talk is a very important tool that can successfully be used to deal with Luci's deceitful tricks. Every moment of the day and night the only person with whom you are with is yourself. Everything you say to yourself impregnates in your mind. "I can do it." "I can't do it." "I'm doing this because I believe I can succeed." "I won't do it because I don't believe I'm going to be successful."

Self-talk is a continuous process, it always goes on and on. Even when you are unconscious about it. You constantly have thoughts circulating in your mind. You constantly receive messages from yourself, they never stop and never going to stop. Every moment of the day you make decisions based on the thoughts you have. Either you are deciding to eat or what clothes to wear, a process of choosing is always taking place.

The choices that you make are based on self-talk.

Self-talk conversation first takes place in the conscious mind. At the first level is what you consciously tell yourself: "I'm good enough" or "I'm not good enough". By repetition, this later translates into what your subconscious mind will retain. The inner conversation is comparable to the background music that plays in a coffee shop or a clothing store. The music plays but you DON'T really listen to it unless you consciously decide to listen.

Even though you don't listen to the music this doesn't mean that it doesn't have an effect on your behavior. It's the same thing when it comes to your thoughts. Even though you might not ACTIVELY listen to your thoughts that don't mean that they don't affect you. Start paying attention to your thoughts. They shape everything in your life. Self-discipline and success are strongly related to the self-talk that you have when you are just with yourself.

Subconsciously, there are debates going on what we impregnate in the mind. Luci hides those debates that are why are not aware of them. This is one of the reasons for which you often find yourself doing things that you were not aware of or intended to. Have you ever said to yourself "I don't know why I did it, I just felt like doing it." Sounds familiar?

When Luci wins a sub conscious talk that is the moment when an action is implemented in your behavior. This is the exact reason why you find yourself doing things that you were really not aware of before. Your behavior is constantly influenced even though you might not be aware of it. When you find yourself having difficulties in being organized it's because of your self-talk which emanates from your subconscious mind.

When you consciously say to yourself "I'm an organized person and I will easily respect my schedule" you have just started a debate. That single sentence is the starting point of a behavior change. Saying that constantly to yourself will just change your actions.

REMEMBER THIS!

Your subconscious mind is influenced by your self-talk. Your words shape everything in your life.

Solution to self-talk

The solution to self-talk is very simple. Have a definite purpose or objective that you are constantly repeating in your mind, through repetition of this thought you will easily recognize behavior that doesn't support your purpose. Luci's influence will go down.

By replacing self-defeating sub conscious messages with positive specific messages, you will find your self-discipline improving tremendously.

The reason we are talking about the importance of self-talk is that you deal with it in every moment of your life. Self-talk becomes even powerful when is combined with action.

What to say to yourself and how to say it?

What you say to yourself must be specific, positive and at present tense. Why? As you have already learned, your subconscious mind believes everything you say to it. Doesn't matter if is good or bad, It will believe it. The subconscious mind understands what happens NOW. Future and past experience don't support you, just the present moment. Whatever message it receives must be stated in the present tense.

"I should start working on my business plan." "I easily work on my business plan right now." Those are two different statements. In the first one, you see the habit of procrastination, of putting aside what you know you should be doing. In the subconscious mind, this is translated in the following way: "I'm not currently working on my business plan." The first affirmation doesn't move you toward working on your business plan. While you are saying to yourself "I should" Luci is sending the message to your conscious mind that a little television won't hurt nobody. Your subconscious mind sends messages to your motor functions, emotions and other physical and psychological network.

If your subconscious mind dictates to yourself to work on your business plan then that's what is going to happen. Your feet, hands and every part of yourself will start working on your business plan in no time. For example, if you are doing something that you don't consider to be the best use of your time. Let's say cleaning your room. Your subconscious mind will ignore it. If every time you clean your room you consider is not the best use of your time this will be noticed by your subconscious mind and will take the form of inaction. As we have already discussed your subconscious mind believes what you tell it without questioning.

REMEMBER THIS!

Repetition is the mother of skill. Repetition is the key to success. The more you repeat a message to yourself, the harder you will start working toward your desires. Is as simple as that! I must say that Luci is good at drifting you away from your path. But with practice, you will be able to recognize what behavior supports your goals and desires in no time!

Remember that when using self-talk, be precise on what you want to be doing now. Be precise and state it as if you are actually already doing it. The rest will be done by your subconscious mind. You will be amazed at what happens when you repeat and reinforce a message to yourself. And also do not forget to positively state to your subconscious mind what you want to do, be or have as if it were already done. Implement that when you are working on your long-term goals and also your short-term goals.

When you say "I can't..." rather than "I consciously choose not to.." you convey to your subconscious mind that you have a choice or not have a choice in that situation. Likewise, when you say "I must.." or "I want to.." you are basically saying to your mind two things. You are first saying to yourself that you don't have options and in the second scenario, you are saying to yourself that, that is your decision. Remember that you always choose. You don't have to do or be anything else except what you decide.

FINAL TIP: Try to start the messages that you want to implement in your subconscious mind aloud. As a result, they will be even stronger because your message will involve speech and hearing. Your messages will be supported by your mental and physical network. Your muscles and motor functions are involved when you are speaking and also when you are hearing. The more parts of yourself you can involve in your self-talk the more powerful will be the message communicated to your subconscious mind. As a result, you will have an easier time implementing anything in your day to day activities. Your self-discipline will start developing easier also.

Chapter 3 – Understanding How Self-Discipline Works

What is self-discipline?

The dictionary definition of self-discipline is as follows: "the ability to control one's feelings and overcome one's weaknesses."

The following are some of the aspects that contribute to a large extent towards lack of self-discipline to individuals:

- Lack of time.
- Lack of money.
- Lack of goals.
- Lack of motivation.
- Habit to procrastinate.
- Lack of organization.
- Lack of focus.
- Lack of recourse.
- Lack of vision.

All the reasons above represent just a snippet of issues when referring to hindrances to self-discipline. It is important to get to the root of the problem, rather than just pursuing changes in behavior that provide only temporary solutions.

It's is worth to bear in mind that, self-discipline is not a personality trait that either you can have it or else you don't have it. It's developed by hours and hours of repeated positive thoughts,behavior or action. Force yourself to overcome your own resistance to action by employing will power.

It's very important to understand what self-discipline represents as well. Self-discipline is the process of coordinating your conscious mind and subconscious mind into doing the action that you desire.

Your personality is a network of different elements. Desires, emotions, needs, thoughts, and imagination all represent different elements of your personality. In all human beings, these elements operate in various degrees of conflict. Sometimes emotions push us in one direction while intellect pulls us in another one. Self-discipline is the skill to direct all the various parts of our personality. Rather than being immobilized by inner conflict, all your mental faculties will be pulling you in a single direction. Self-discipline represents a psychological self-management process, rather than a personality trait. You can think of self-discipline as a film director. The film director just gives instructions to actors and they execute.

Key to self-discipline

It doesn't matter if you trying to attract the right partner in your life, to stick to your diet, to clean your room or to be more productive, the success revolves around your ability to control yourself. Since you were young until you reached maturity you have always been told what to do. Your parents told you what to eat and how to dress. Your teachers told you what to learn and what you have to do for the next class. Your piano teacher told you which keys to press and how you have to practice.

Since you were a little kid you have been told what the next step is. When you got a job your boss told you what your tasks are. Discipline was something that somebody directed on you. You didn't have to manage your own actions and to take decisions. Usually, we are told what to do, how to do it and also when to do it. You didn't have to be 100% responsible for your life because it has been guided by others.

Having that said, we didn't have to struggle to develop our inner force. It takes willpower to create self-discipline, vision, and motivation to follow your plan or to create one. Therefore our self-discipline doesn't have the opportunity to get exercised. Whatever is not used is not kept. Without exercise, your self-discipline weakens. The downside is that in situations where we need to have discipline is hard to exorcist that because you don't have it.

Because we spent so much time of our lives been guided by others, we no longer develop such skills. Self-discipline is like a muscle. As you train your muscles in the gym and make them grown is also how you develop your self-discipline. By reinforcing ideas constantly, you will have an easier time doing the things that you plan. As time goes by, certain psychological roadblocks occur that inhibit the development of self-discipline, so be sure that you start to discipline yourself as soon as possible.

Dig as deep as possible in yourself!

When you start developing self-discipline you will have to face certain realities about yourself. You don't have to ignore these realities and I suggest you shouldn't ignore your current situation either. You have to be completely honest about your current situation before planning or trying to make a change in your life. Don't be surprised if you encounter fear as being the biggest problem in your self-development process.

Fear is such an amazing motivator but also an enemy. A small degree of fear in what you are doing is absolutely ok. We tend to act more from the fear of suffering than from seeking pleasure. As a result, fear can help you but also can be your enemy. If the fear is too much you will be paralyzed and have a hard time taking action. This will produce procrastination, poor work, poor time management and also you will find yourself avoiding tasks. The result will be lack of self-discipline. As I have mentioned certain fear create roadblocks in your path.

If we dig deep to root out this fear we will find out that:

-	Facing your fear creates anxiety.
-	Since we were kids we have been conditioned to view fear as a bad thing, as a result 	the rationalization of "I'm afraid"
-	We were conditioned to view fear as a weakness.

Until you become aware of your own fears and what is preventing you from taking action you will continue to lack self-discipline. Being aware of your fears and accepting them is a part of being human. You will never be able to escape fear, just to accept it. Subconscious fears will prevent you from taking action. Below I've enumerated the most troublesome and common fears that block us from developing self-discipline. We are all subjected to a kind of fear in various degrees.

The more you know about them, the easier will be for you to minimize their influence:

- Fear of success.
- Fear of rejection.
- Fear of failure.
- Fear of criticism.
- Fear of loss.
- Fear of mediocrity.

All those fears are created by the idea that everything we experience will create suffering. It's our conditions as human beings to try to avoid pain and suffering. Our brain considers that pain and suffering can jeopardize our existence even though has been the number one reason for which we evolved as species.

We will continue to explore more in the next chapters.

Chapter 4 – Systems to develop Self-discipline

Fear of failure

It is nothing new the fact that all of us experienced fear of failure. Fear of failure is one of the common forms of fears that you will encounter. Studies have revealed that this kind of fear is the greatest obstacle to personal success. Even though a large number of people want success just a few people really achieve it. Fear of failure may be the greatest obstacle to personal success. Isn't that surprising? Even though we all want success we are stopped by concerns? What most of us don't realize in this life is that these fears are not real. Most of them are based on a self-defeating misconception.

Most people don't pursue their deepest desires, which are caused by past failures, which are located in corners of our subconscious. The emotion of pain is too strong that sometimes just stops us from taking action. Sometimes if this fear is correctly used it can bring the most out of a person.

But why do we tend to see failure as something bad? Why do we tend to stay away from pain? We have the tendency to connect failed endeavor to our self-esteem. That is one of the biggest reasons we prefer to stay away from the emotion of failure. We take the activity that we have to do as being something personal. We imply ego in activities that we do and attach it to the outcome. "I've failed in doing business so I'm a failure." "I failed in this relationship so I'm not worthy enough to have that girl." "I failed again." Probably you have had these affirmations in your life on several occasions, we subconsciously tell them to ourselves. At this point, I will emphasize the importance of self-talk as we have already discussed to remind you once again how crucial it is to pay attention to what you tell to yourself.

You are not your failure as you are not your success. You are just yourself. The failure or the success is just your perception. Even though authors like Napoleon Hill say things like "Success is the progressive realization of a worthy ideal" is not recommended to identify yourself with what you are doing. Sure you might fail at what you are doing. You can fail to deliver your project on time or you can fail losing weight or to make a certain amount of money. Yes, it can happen and probably happened to everybody who failed at some point in their lives. But that doesn't make you a failure. It's just the attempt that failed. You got that option out. You now have other options to try and test. You are not a failure if you failed.

The fear of failure contributes to our lack of self-discipline.

REMEMBER THIS!

Think about Thomas Edison. Before succeeding in inventing the light bulb he failed over 1000 times. Did this make Edison a failure? Absolutely not. Edison saw each failure as something that took him closer to inventing the light bulb. His attitude was essential to continue trying. Edison's experience with the light bulb demonstrates the absurdity of linking failure to self-esteem. I guess we can say that Edison "saw the light at the end of the tunnel".

Our egos have been trained to be like that. Society, friends, parents or school trained us to think that to fail is something bad. To fail is something to be ashamed of. As a result, we grew more reluctant to attempt anything at which we are not guaranteed of success. It has been implanted in our subconscious mind thoughts like: "If I fail, they will laugh at me." "If I fail, they will see me as a fool."

The fact is that those thoughts are going into the subconscious mind and we are not aware of it. We are not aware of how powerful is their influence on our behavior. This causes our self-discipline to weaken. The truth is that if we are going to fail in anything we try for the first time, it does not mean that it will fail for the second time as long as we don't repeat the mistakes of the past.

Because of this type of thinking it is easier for many people to continue compulsive drinking, eating, smoking or indulging in any type of activity that doesn't support them. They don't risk being humiliated because they don't try anything risky.

Think about an athlete who is procrastinating. An athlete who can't get himself to promptly perform the tasks required to be at his best. In most of those cases, the fear of failure is what keeps him from taking action. And please have in mind that there are a lot of people in that situation (I have been in that situation many times before writing this book). The athlete that procrastinates is like a business man who is scared of investing money because he might lose it. He is subconsciously telling himself that if he fails, he won't be respected, he will be humiliated.

He is also coming into a discussion about the fear of success. If he succeeds in what he tries he will be wrong. He will be wrong about what he believed until that moment. This will interrupt the self-image that he had until that moment. That won't be related to what he thought about himself and how he saw himself until that moment. I hope you also can see how those two are related.

The same logic operates with students who can't get themselves to study or complete assignments on time. This is strongly related to their attitude. This attitude provides a shield against humiliations that later is translated in how they behave at their jobs or their business if they decide to start a business.

Before self-discipline can be employed we have to accept our selves. Fear of failure must be accepted. We must accept that failure is something very normal, there is nothing wrong to fail and to love the process. When we drag fear of failure out into the light, we'll find that humiliation is the brick that constructs the foundation of lack of self-discipline and lack of success. In any moment of our life, we must remind ourselves that failure is not something wrong. Failure is not humiliation unless we decide to see it like that in our minds. Failure is just something that takes us closer to our goal. Once you fully accept this fact you will be free of fear. Don't get me wrong fear will always exist somewhere inside of your mind (remember Luci). But now you have control of it. Fear of failure loses its power. As a result of that, it will slowly stop sabotaging your self-discipline.

REMEMBER THIS!

Failure is not humiliation! Failure is representing humiliation if WE DECIDE to see it like that. Every action that we take, takes the form that we decide to give it. Failure is just a stepping stone to our success.

Don't let fear inhibit you. You can see now the importance of minimizing the power of fear. For you to reduce the power that fear of failure has over you, you have to refuse the link of failure to your self-esteem.

Solution to fear of failure

Take a piece of paper. Write all the things that you want to try in future, not goals, write down only activities, business ideas that you have and so on. After that write what is stopping you from pursuing each of those activities. After that, I strongly suggest you to write down things that you were afraid in past and what kept you from taking action.

Fear of success

You might be surprised to hear about fear of success but it's real. Fear of success is as real as fear of failure. As the well know author Napoleon Hill puts it "Success is the progressive realization of a worthy ideal". You might ask yourself why fear success? How can you fear being the desired person?

We tend to see the bad side of everything. As we can see the fear of failure as it exists in our lives we can also see the fear of success. Subconsciously, our feelings regarding the negative side of success are very much alive. Having a subconscious negative perception about success can make you not to try to achieve it anymore. Our self-discipline weakens again. A subconscious part of us does not really want to be successful. Being successful would mean for us to be responsible, would mean to assume the new person that you are representing right now. A lot of complications are implied, why bother?

We are powerless to fight with the fear of success if we are not aware of our subconscious mind. We all have at least one friend that we know that is sabotaging his/her success. We all know one person that seems to do everything possible to keep himself/herself away from his goal. How weird is that? To want to achieve something but in the same time to act in ways that will keep you away from your dream. And the craziest part is that this is representing just another form of fear.

"Maybe I don't really need to be that good." "Maybe I'm not worthy of this car." "Maybe I don't really deserve to be successful." Feeling of guilt is also implied. Feeling of embarrassment, feeling of shame and the list can go on. Having this type of view over life will just reveal a very low self-esteem. Telling yourself that you don't deserve to be happy is not showing self-confidence also. To tell yourself that you are not worthy of accomplishing big goals, having great relationships and an amazing health will just lower and lower your self-esteem. Why is this happening? Usually, this happens when the unfulfilled expectation of others are being created. Here I'm talking about family friends or lover.

There is also another side that you can identify when we talk about fear of success. "If I'm successful, people will talk and they won't like me anymore." By being feared due to success you will discover how strongly this is related to the fear of criticism. Many people fear success just because they won't be able to identify with their group of friends.

They would have to feel the pressure of living with the success. Absolutely amazing, right?

After you start being good at something people will start to have expectations. Now that you are a great Painter you have to keep it up. Your next painting must be even better than the previous one, right? "Now everyone is going to expect my next work to be even better." This thought is just putting even pressure on you. Is this helping you? Absolutely not. Just get things logical. How could you even be able to perform better if you are living with this fear? "The top is pretty lonely." You might be thinking: How will they react to my success?

Subconsciously we tell ourselves that when success enters in our life we are going to experiment pain and suffering. At the end of the day don't forget that pain and suffering are what we ultimately try to avoid. But please be conscious that those thoughts are not real. We imagine the pressure that doesn't exist. We imagine overwhelming responsibilities that also doesn't exist. Subconsciously we know that having success, along with the way we are going to develop self-discipline. We are going to do things that we are 100% comfortable.

Solution to fear of success

Take a piece of paper. Write your past experiences where you had success. Also, add what problems those experiences create for yourself. As you write your experiences, please emphasize what kind of problems you had. What kept you away from success. I suggest you to be as specific as possible.

Fear of rejection

Since we were little children we were looking for our parent's approval. We were looking for our friends to like us or to get validated by the loved ones. Unfortunately, this mentality didn't change. Due to the fact that we seek approval, fear of rejection became dominant in many aspects of our lives. If we don't keep an eye on it, our desire for approval may paralyze us, as much as any other form of fear.

This kind of fear affects a lot self-discipline. Boys usually during childhood and adolescence trying to please their fathers. This creates traumatic feelings and loneliness that can haunt that person for many years.

Fear of rejection can generate a feeling of inferiority and turn you in a person with the defensive attitude towards life. A person who subconsciously fears rejection doesn't see it as being fear. For that person, fear is something normal to worry about it. Rejection looks like something normal. People who fear rejection are perceived as pleasing others. The fear of being rejected makes them tolerate bad behavior of the people around them. To develop self-discipline, you will have to overcome feelings of anxiety and insecurity. You will have to say "No" more often than you will have to say "Yes" to people asking you for favors. Indeed, people might not like you, not all the people you meet might not like you. I want to remind you that your job is not to be liked by everybody. Your job is to live the best life that you can.

Whether you are getting a "No" from a job application or a "No" from your friends, fear of rejection shouldn't bother you. Fear of rejection keeps us from being disciplined. Due to the fact that we feel as if someone is constantly looking over to you to judge you. This causes us to judge our self and to feel guilty about our choices.

Solution to fear of rejection

On a piece of paper explore your past experiences that made you feel bad about rejection. Write down situation where your behavior was based on a fear of being rejected by family or friends. Take in consideration experience from earliest memories also. As you are writing ask yourself how this affected you physically or emotionally.

Fear of mediocrity

When you spend over ten years writing your book do you think you are being a perfectionist or you fear of publishing a mediocre book? Probably the answer is your fear of publishing a mediocre book. Perfectionism is not what is keeping you away from being at your best is the fear of being mediocre.

If you take a look at how perfectionism looks like would you be able to recognize it? Would you be able to measure it or define it? I'm pretty sure that you won't be able to do that. You will discover that is a sort of a standard imposed by society. The idea of perfectionism is representing the subconscious fear of looking mediocre. We don't want to look mediocre to our self or to others. Attempting to be perfectionist will make us procrastinate or not have the courage to take action. This fear is just another way of making our self-discipline weaker.

This type of fear produces also anxiety and many mental diseases. People usually find relief by drinking alcohol or abusing drugs. This type of fear sends to our subconscious mind the following message: "My efforts might not be rewarded at the right level. I should avoid doing X activity until is perfect." As I said, as a result of that our self-discipline and self-esteem has to suffer. We must accept fear, not to try to fight with it. Regardless of our chosen task, we might find ourselves in a situation like the following: " If I can't do it as perfect as possible, then I won't do it at all." Chasing perfection is like chasing shadows. It is a projection of your imagination.

REMEMBER THIS!

None of us is perfect, you should not fear mediocrity but also not to aspire to it. At the end of the day, we are all human and is important to accept you as you are.

Solution to fear of mediocrity

On a piece of paper write your past experiences that made you feel bad about mediocrity. Write down what caused that and how you felt physically and emotionally. It's important to write down any kind of action that was based on fear of not doing something good enough.

Fear of taking risks

For many of us, safety and security are just normal things. We feel the need of being secure financially, emotionally or physically. In areas where we have difficulties with our self-discipline, we are going beyond what we desire or what we consider as being right to us. Like the rest of our fears, fear of risks operates from the subconscious mind. Fear of taking risks is subtle. Fear of taking risks manipulates you and as a result, this leads to stagnation in your life.

We may have a feeling that we are comfortable. This often can be a false idea. This is caused just by the desire not to take risks or to take as few as possible. Life became very boring when we don't embrace risks and challenges. Life becomes routine when we view risks as being dangerous or view them as something bad. Instead, we could see risks as an opportunity for growth. You also might ask yourself, how fear of risk is lowering your self-discipline.

Researchers have found out that those people who fear taking risks are the people who are unable to succeed in unknown situation. You might say to yourself, well that pretty obvious, so what? Well, the important thing is that they have a hard time focusing on the fact that unknown situation doesn't have to be something bad. When self-doubt intrudes your self-discipline it becomes very hard to say to yourself "I can make it happen". Self-talk importance being emphasized again.

The connection between self-confidence and self-discipline might appear to be pretty loose but it's very important. Self-Discipline is a collection composed of many diverse psychological forces which add up to a larger force. Moreover, our self-discipline gains strength just by constant repetition. Constant repetition and exercise that leans heavily on self-discipline.

When people stop taking risks their self-confidence muscle, won't be usable when you want to use it. As a result, self-confidence is one of the most important elements of self-discipline. If a person refrains from taking risks, JUST FOR A SHORT TIME, a subconscious fear of taking risks will come into his/her mind.

REMEMBER THIS!

Self-confidence supports self-discipline. Develop self-confidence and you will develop your self-discipline. Self-discipline can be hindered by fear of risks. This fear can be overcome just by changing your attitude. Everything is under your control!

Solution to fear of taking risks

On a piece of paper write your past experiences that made you not to take action due to fear of risks. Write down what caused that and how you felt physically and emotionally in those situations. It's important to write down any kind of action that was based on a fear of not taking risks.

Before going further, always be aware of the existence of these five fears. Don't forget that within all humans being these fears are present. They develop over time and take different forms. You will never get rid of fear, but that is a good thing. Fear will keep you on track of your life. The five most important fears are as follows:

- Fear of failure.
- Fear of success.

-   Fear of rejection.
-   Fear of mediocrity.
-   Fear of risks.

Chapter 5 – Subconscious belief systems

Subconscious belief systems

As you learn more about this subject you will begin to develop an awareness of the underlying attitudes and beliefs that created the subconscious fears about which you have been studying in this book. Each of the fears presented may seem irrational. But the reality is that they have a very strong base in your subconscious mind. These attitudes and beliefs determine our daily actions and also in actions.

It's important to know and to be conscious of the fact that most of our beliefs operate subconsciously. Before trying to change past behaviors you must be aware of the current ones. You must be aware of their existence. In order to improve your self-discipline, you need to be able to change beliefs that don't support your goals.

Subconscious beliefs inhibit the development of self-discipline. Self-discipline has four main stages:
1. The decision to take action.
2. Preparation.
3. Action.
4. Constant work to maintain the result.

A lot of people start developing self-discipline by going directly to the Action stage. They overlook decision to act and preparation. That's why you put aside that project that you been telling yourself that you will do soon.

Many people begin new year with calendars-plans but after a couple of weeks or days, they stop. Jumping directly to Action stage without deciding clearly what you want to do and preparation for it won't support your goals.

REMEMBER THIS!

Self-discipline is developed over time. It takes effort, practice, and repetition to develop it. It's a process with steps and stages.

"There is just one way to do things." "Either you do it right or don't do it at all. "My point of view is the best one."

The preceding statements represent a belief that comes from past self-defeating behavior. Life is lived in a grey area. It's lived somewhere between black and white. It's lived somewhere between good or bad. It's not recommended to say that things are just in a way and can't be changed. Nothing lasts forever.

"All or nothing" is an affirmation that keeps gambling a lot of people from taking action or taking the right action. They end up not doing anything. Extremist's attitudes reveal many of the subconscious fears we previously developed. Also, the "all or nothing" attitude paralyzes our efforts of getting ourselves into developing a strong self-discipline.

That also happens because we subconsciously have developed fear of taking risks, under this belief system a lot more than you can imagine. Success, for the most part, means living a life free of fear, organized and dedicated to constant work and constant improvement. But most people are not willing to do that even though are constantly thinking about success. How interesting is that, right?

If you define yourself only as a champ or a chump then starting new habits will be very hard for you. When starting something new you will always be a chump until you become a champ. If you tell yourself that if your plan doesn't work then you are a loser it's one of the biggest mistakes you can make. "All or nothing" means to work against yourself. This inner battle will drain you of the energy necessary to perseverance toward any goal. "All or nothing" thinking is very strongly related to subconscious fears that you developed over time.

Visualization

When it comes to behavior change visualization is one of the most powerful tools that you can use. Visualization is one of the easiest and most effective tools for developing self-discipline. The best part about visualization is that it requires only your imagination. It's limited just by what you dream and what you want and can create in your mind. You tend to visualize pleasant experiences and also unpleasant experiences. You do it when you remember something from your past or when you create something for your future. Visualization is used all the time to create a shape in your mind to what you want to bring in the physical world. Subconsciously you use visualization hundreds of times during a day. So, how does this relate to self-discipline?

All your actions and non-actions are related to the mental images that you create about your chosen goal. When you decide on a new goal visualization helps you to create an image in your mind of how the first result you want to look like. Your mental images will either support your efforts or will oppose your efforts.

REMEMBER THIS!

Negative thoughts and images can consciously be changed into positive images. Visualization is also a result of your self-talk that uses mental pictures instead of words. Please be aware of the fact that you can visualize positive thoughts and also negative thoughts. As you bring to reality positive thoughts you can bring to reality negative ones. Be aware of what you visualize. Visualizing yourself not being happy, not happy with the person you want in your life can take form as easy as a positive thought.

In the previous chapters, we talked about self-talk and the importance of the way you talk to yourself. We talked about that words play a big role in your self-discipline efforts. Concrete words and phrases support or oppose your goals. But words represent just a part of the way you can influence your subconscious mind.

Visualization is self-talk in the form of images. Self-defeating mental images won't support your goals and those need to be replaced with supportive mental images. When you choose a goal you instantly create a mental image with the final result. You start creating an image on how your body would look like if you want to change the way you look. If you want a new relationship in your life you start visualizing how that person would look like and how would behave.

Consciously choose to create vivid mental movies that involve your goal. For example, if you plan to wake up earlier to go to gym visualize that. Every day before rising earlier visualize yourself going to the gym. See yourself stretching and lifting weights. Feel the iron, feel how you lift it. Is important to include as many details to your visualization as you can. Create image as vivid and as complex as possible.

Before going into action on your project, each day visualize yourself in action as often as you can. Ten times, twenty times, a hundred times daily, as many as you can. It only takes you a couple of seconds to do it. Close your eyes for a couple of seconds and entertain your goals and positive thoughts with your mind. Practice visualization every day for a week, before you jump into action. Decide on what you want, in this case going to the gym in the morning. After that prepare yourself and take action. By doing that you gain self-discipline that will support changing your self-image and will make your weaknesses disappear.

Visualization prior to action will bring up your commitment to do that you set for yourself to do! Increase your confidence, validate your ability to motivate you and many other useful abilities will come to the surface. By the simple act of visualizing yourself doing and being the person, you want to be will minimize your subconscious fears and doubts. Visualization will bring into your subconscious mind "the new you".

REMEMBER THIS!

Visualize as clearly as you can your desired outcome. Visualize all the specific details of the activity you want to do. See, smell, feel, hear, touch it, everything you can do imagine in your mind. Make it real in your mind and you will make it real in reality.

Chapter 6 – Taking Control of Yourself

"Some people just won't change." "This is just the way I am, I can't change." "I'm just like my father, can't do nothing about that." "I can't change myself."

How sad is when you hear people making those affirmations. Even worst is when they think that for themselves and totally consider it. People do change. They really can change and become the person that they want. No one can't change and become somebody a new person. The desire to change must come from within. If a person wants to change then that person needs to *choose to change*. Consciously and subconsciously that person has to choose to change. Increasing one's self-discipline will qualify as a change. This applies regardless of whether the self-discipline will be put to use with a small project or with a big project.

Our behavior, emotions, intellect and everything else about us are as a result of our choices. Most of these choices are made on a daily basis. Daily we decide whether to continue current actions that we have chosen for our self. The choice is what links our current behavior to our past decisions, experiences, and influences.

If you want to be chained to your past you will be as long as you choose to be. "That's how I've been for last ten years, I can't change." "You can't teach old dog new tricks." Those type of affirmations will reflect an unwillingness to accept responsibility for your current life.

Don't allow your yesterday decisions and actions to dictate your today's choices. Keep in mind that with a positive attitude you can put yourself in the right state of mind to take action. The reverse is also true if you put yourself in a negative state of mind. You are now gaining information's and techniques to make the change of your life. Choose wisely what you want to focus on because that will shape you. Be prepared for when the opportunity appears by making the right decisions.

Conclusion

Thank you again for downloading this book!

I hope this book was able to help you to understand how self discipline affects us and also enjoyed the book!

The next step is to be sure that you fully understand the information, also apply it and read it as frequently as necessary.

Finally, if you enjoyed this book, then I'd like to ask you for a favour, would you be kind enough to leave a review for this book on Amazon? It'd be greatly appreciated!

* 9 7 8 1 9 7 7 7 8 1 4 3 7 *